TEACH YOURSELF TO PLAY

GUITAR CHORDS

by Steve Gorenberg

Don't delay, start today!

This book provides a quick, effective, uncomplicated, and practical method to playing guitar chords. Get started right away and learn at your own pace in the comfort of your home.

To access audio, visit:
www.halleonard.com/mylibrary

Enter Code
5539-4165-2596-3045

Other *Teach Yourself to Play Guitar* books

00696029

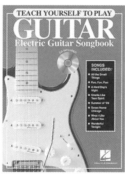

00699791

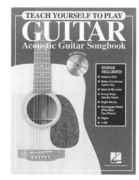

00699792

ISBN 978-1-4950-1691-2

Visit Hal Leonard Online at
www.halleonard.com

World headquarters, contact:
Hal Leonard
7777 West Bluemound Road
Milwaukee, WI 53213
Email: info@halleonard.com

In Europe, contact:
Hal Leonard Europe Limited
1 Red Place
London, W1K 6PL
Email: info@halleonardeurope.com

In Australia, contact:
Hal Leonard Australia Pty. Ltd.
4 Lentara Court
Cheltenham, Victoria, 3192 Australia
Email: info@halleonard.com.au

Introduction

Congratulations on your decision to learn how to play guitar! This book is a perfect introduction to the world of guitar chords. If you've never played guitar or any other instrument, *Teach Yourself to Play Guitar Chords* is an excellent place to begin, and doesn't require you to have any prior musical experience. You'll be able to start playing right away, without having to learn how to read traditional music. The examples in this book are all presented in an easy-to-follow system designed specifically for beginner guitar.

This book begins with some basic guitar knowledge, the parts of the guitar, how to tune, how to hold the guitar, and how to read chord diagrams—just the very basics to get you started. Then we'll dive right into the playing! By the time you get through the second chapter, you'll already know enough guitar chords to play hundreds of songs. As you progress through the book, you'll learn how to read guitar tab, along with a simple rhythmic notation system. There are included songs to play, and many other examples to help you master guitar chords and strumming, all with the help of the recorded tracks so you can hear exactly how everything should sound.

The objective is to get you started playing immediately. Be patient and take your time in the beginning, reviewing each example to make sure that you've got it down before moving on. Once you've learned the beginning major and minor chords and can change chords smoothly, you'll be well on your way. Then we'll continue with movable chords, power chords, suspensions, and barre chords—all without having to read music or learn a lot of theory and scales. By the time you get through this book, you'll be equipped with the knowledge you need to continue learning and growing as a guitarist long after you've mastered everything presented here. Most of all, go have fun!

Table of Contents

Chapter 1
The Basics

Parts of the Guitar

The basic components on an acoustic guitar or an electric guitar are the same. The main difference between them is how they produce sound. An acoustic guitar has a large, hollow body to amplify the sound. An electric guitar uses pickups like a microphone to capture the strings' vibrations and send the signal to an amplifier.

The three basic sections of the guitar are the body, the neck, and the headstock. The front face of the neck is often referred to as the fretboard or fingerboard. The headstock contains the tuning keys (also called machine heads), which are used to tune the strings. The parts of the guitar that will be occasionally referenced throughout this book are labeled below.

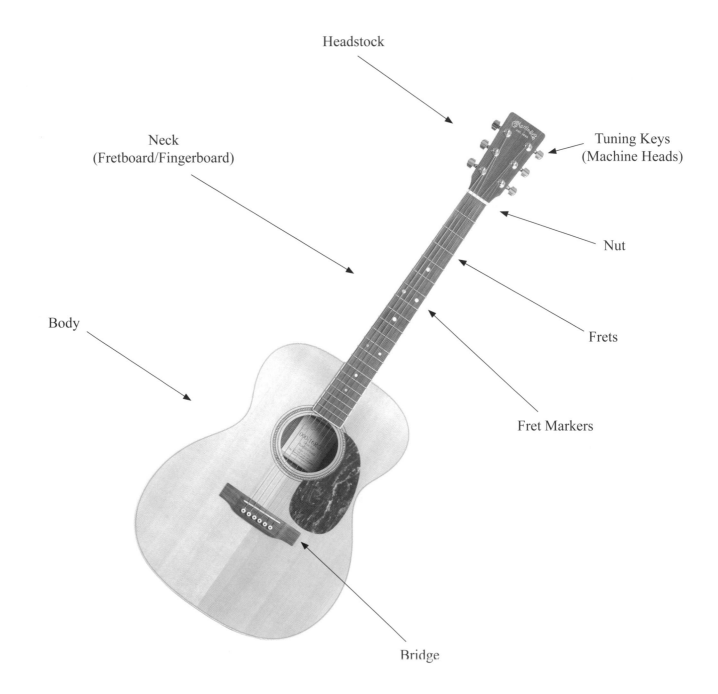

Headstock

Neck
(Fretboard/Fingerboard)

Tuning Keys
(Machine Heads)

Nut

Body

Frets

Fret Markers

Bridge

Left-hand Position

Keep your left hand relaxed and your fingers arched. The first joint of your thumb and your fingertips are the only parts of your hand that should be touching the guitar. Avoid gripping the neck like a baseball bat; your palm should not be touching the guitar neck.

Place the first joint of your thumb on the back of the guitar neck.

Curl your fingers so that only your fingertips are touching the strings.

Holding the Pick

Hold the pick in your right hand by gripping it firmly between your thumb and first finger. Keep the rest of your hand relaxed and your fingers slightly curved and out of the way. You can pick the strings in a downward motion using a *downstroke*, or in an upward motion using an *upstroke*. Most of the time, you'll be combining the two in an alternating down-up-down-up motion. While picking single notes, the motion should come from your wrist. While strumming chords, keep your wrist straight and let the motion come from your elbow.

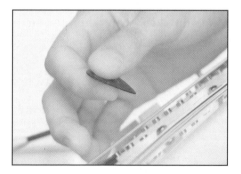

Many exercises in this book will include a series of arrows under the music to indicate downstrokes and upstrokes.

Downstroke   Upstroke

Tuning

The strings on the guitar are tuned in order from the lowest-sounding (thickest) string to the highest-sounding (thinnest) string. The lowness or highness of a note is called *pitch*. The six guitar strings are tuned to specific pitches when played *open* (no fingers pressing them down). In order, from lowest to highest, the pitches of the open strings are: E, A, D, G, B, and E. The highest-sounding (thinnest) string is referred to as the 1st string; the lowest-sounding (thickest) string is referred to as the 6th string.

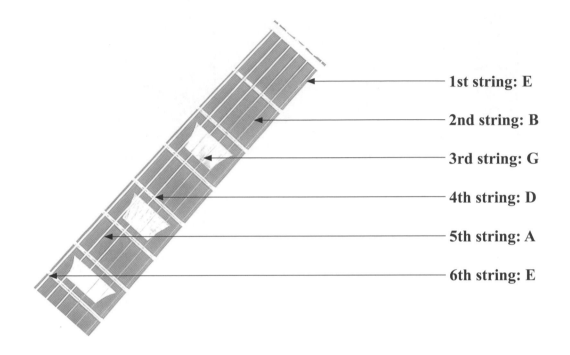

- 1st string: E
- 2nd string: B
- 3rd string: G
- 4th string: D
- 5th string: A
- 6th string: E

A guitar is tuned by using the tuning pegs to tighten or loosen the strings. There are a few methods you can use to tune the strings, but electronic tuners, computer software, and smartphone apps are all available to make it easier for you. Always turn the peg slowly and gradually. Even if you're using a tuner or app, try to use your ear to get the string in the ballpark so you can avoid over-tightening and accidentally breaking the string. If you're tuning by ear (to another instrument, guitar, or recording), get the string close to the correct pitch, then begin listening for a series of pulsating beats that should slow down and eventually stop when the string is in tune. Once your ear is trained to hear differences in pitches, tuning will become easier.

The photos below show which string corresponds to each tuning peg on two popular types of headstocks.

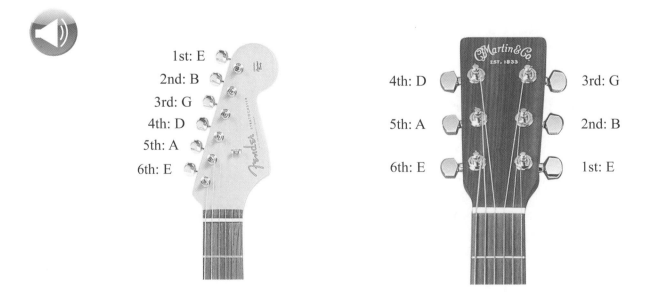

Chord Diagrams

Chords are taught in this book by using graphic representations of the fretboard called *chord diagrams*. The vertical lines in the diagrams represent the strings; the horizontal lines represent the frets. The thick horizontal line at the top of the diagram represents the nut. Chord diagrams visually correspond to the guitar as if you stood the guitar up from floor to ceiling and looked directly at the fretboard.

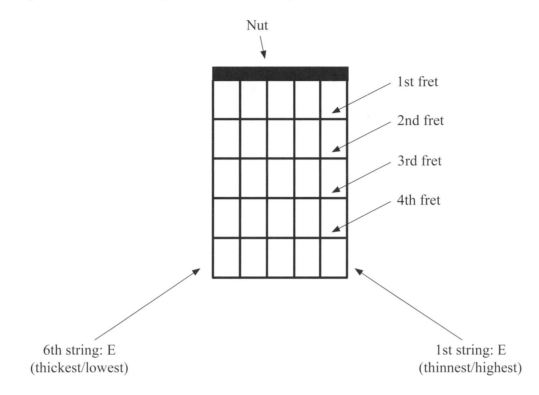

The letters above the chord diagrams represent the chord names. The black dots on the diagram indicate which notes are fretted (pressed down) with fingers. A number is assigned to each finger of your left hand (1 = index, 2 = middle, 3 = ring, 4 = pinky), and the fingering for each chord is shown underneath the chord diagram. The O's above the diagrams indicate which strings are played or strummed open (with no fingers touching them). An X above the diagram indicates that the string should be muted or not played.

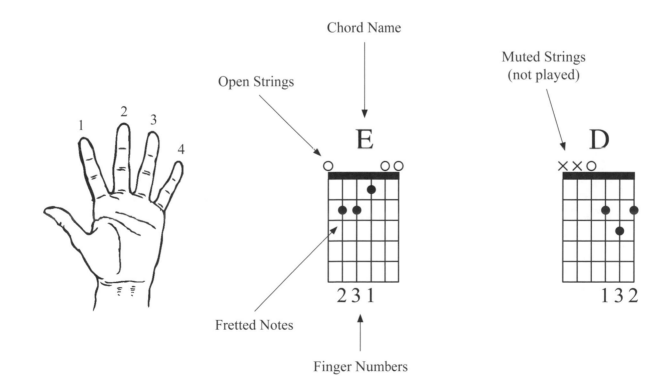

Chord Charts

A series of chords played in a specific order is called a *chord progression*. Instead of using traditional music notation, guitar chord progressions are often written out in a chord chart, with the chord names shown above a musical staff. Chord charts show the guitarist the rhythm or count for the song, and show when to change chords. Written music is divided into *measures* (or bars) that are counted in rhythm. Most modern rock and blues is played in 4/4 time (four beats per measure). When a band counts off the beat at the beginning of a song ("One, two, three, four"), it represents one measure of music in 4/4 time.

The 4/4 fraction at the beginning of the example below tells us that the music is in 4/4 time. This is called a *time signature*. The music is divided into measures via vertical *barlines*. The example below is four measures long. The barline at the end is a double barline, indicating that the example is over. The chords are shown above the staff, and the diagonal slashes written on the staff are simply there as a reference—to show you where the beats are located.

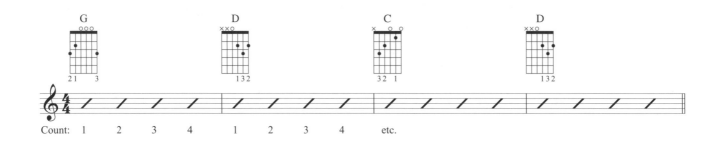

Tablature

Tablature (or *tab*) is another system for notating guitar music without using traditional notes. A tab staff consists of six horizontal lines, each line representing a string on the guitar. The lowest line represents the lowest-pitched string (6th string), and the highest line represents the highest-pitched string (1st string). The numbers placed on the string lines refer to fret numbers on the guitar. If a "0" is used, it means the string should be played open (not fretted). If an "X" is used, then the string should be muted. Chords are represented in tab by stacking the numbers on top of each other.

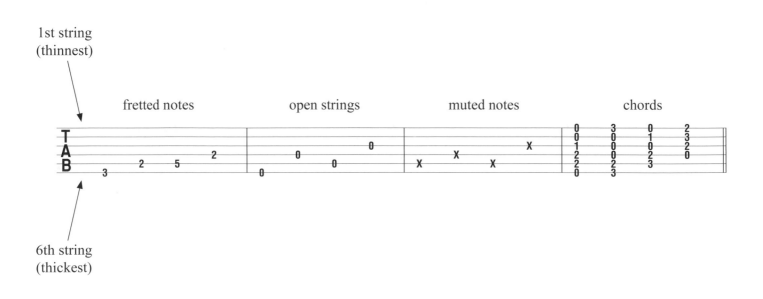

Chapter 2
Open-position Major and Minor Chords

Let's get started with the most popular major and minor chords. All of the following chords are referred to as *open-position* chords because they contain open strings and are played within the lowest part of the fretboard. These are the most commonly used guitar chords and they form the basis for thousands of songs. In this chapter, we'll learn how to play these basic open chords, and practice changing from one chord to the next. This will give you a good foundation for playing countless simple songs.

The two most basic types of chords are *major chords* and *minor chords*. Major chords have a bright, happy sound; minor chords have a darker, more melancholy sound. A lowercase "m" is used in a chord name to indicate that the chord is minor.

Em Chord

The open E minor chord is one of the easiest chords to play on the guitar because all six strings are strummed and only two left-hand fingers are needed to fret the necessary notes. Using the chord diagram below as a guide, place your second finger at the second fret of the fifth string, and your third finger at the second fret of the fourth string. Using only your fingertips, press against the strings firmly while keeping the rest of your hand and wrist relaxed. Your fingers should be curled so that no other part of your hand touches the other strings. Position your fingers slightly before the fret (between the first and second frets) as shown in the photo. If you place your fingers too close to the second fret, the notes will buzz and you won't get a clear, sustained tone.

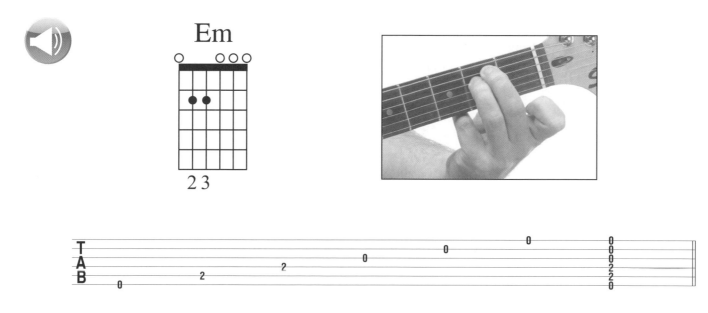

To make sure that you're properly fretting the chord, pick each string individually from low to high as shown in the tab staff above. If the notes on the fourth and fifth strings are muted or buzzing, then you're not pressing down firmly enough. This may feel difficult at first, but it shouldn't take long to get used to. If your thumb is positioned properly on the back of the neck and you direct the energy of your fingertips just right, it should take very little effort to get a clean-sounding note. Make sure your fingers aren't accidentally touching the other strings. If the open third string sounds muted or deadened, then part of your third finger is accidentally touching it and you'll have to slightly readjust your fingers. The first joint of each finger should be perpendicular to the neck, pressing inward against the fretboard.

E Chord

The open E major chord is similar to the Em chord, with only one additional finger needed to fret the chord. With your second and third fingers in the same place they were for the Em chord, add your first finger to the first fret of the third string as shown in the chord diagram below. Pick each note individually to make sure that they're all ringing out properly. If the note on the third string sounds muted or deadened, then you might be accidentally touching it with your third finger. If the second string sounds muted, then your first finger may need to be adjusted.

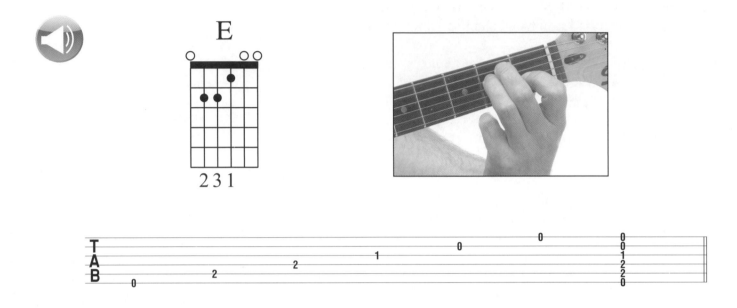

Am Chord

The open A minor chord uses the same fingers as the open E major chord above, but every finger is moved up one string so that your fingers are fretting the notes on the second, third, and fourth strings. Notice the "X" above the sixth string in the chord diagram. This indicates that the sixth string is not played, and you should only strum from the fifth to the first strings.

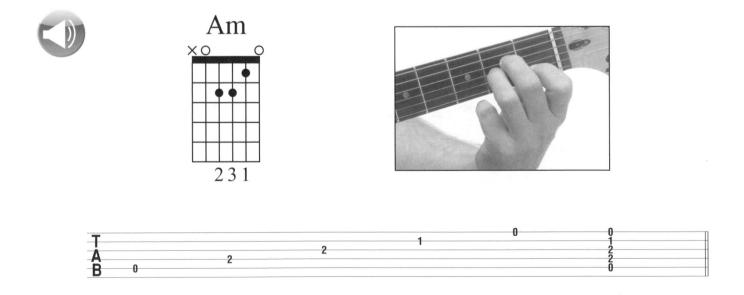

Now let's try changing from chord to chord. The more you practice changing chords, the easier it will become, and your fingers will instinctively move into position. In the example below, play steady downstrokes, switching between the E and Am chords where indicated. Try moving your fingers together in one smooth motion when changing chords, rather than repositioning each finger one at a time. It's essential to learn how to change chords seamlessly and in time without pausing.

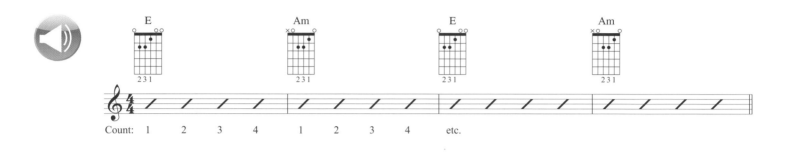

C Chord

To play the open C major chord, you'll need to stretch your fingers across three frets. Make sure that your third finger is reaching far enough into the third fret to get a clean note that isn't buzzing or muted. As with the other chords, be sure that your fingers aren't accidentally touching and muting the strings below them. You may be tempted to angle your hand slightly for this chord, but keep your fingers as perpendicular to the strings as possible. Only the first joint of your thumb should be pressing against the back of the neck. If the heel of your thumb is pressed against the neck, your fingers will be too angled to achieve clean, sustainable notes.

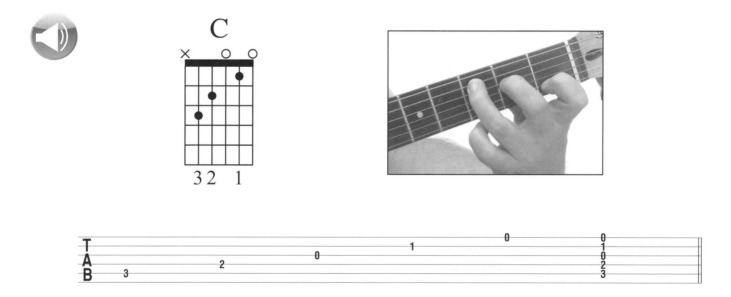

Now let's try changing from the C to the Am chord. If you compare the fingerings, you'll notice that only the third finger needs to move. When switching between the two chords, instead of taking your whole hand off the fretboard, try leaving your first and second fingers in place, moving just your third finger in a single, smooth motion.

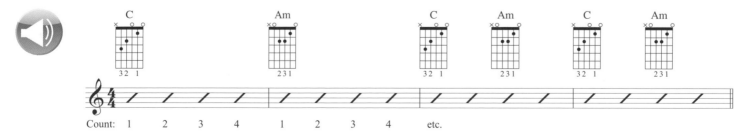

G Chord

The open G major chord is strummed on all six strings and uses the first, second, and third fingers to fret the notes.

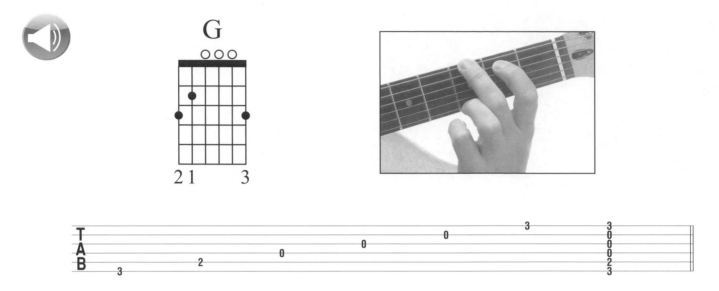

Let's try changing from the G chord to the Em chord. Sometimes you can slightly alter the fingering of a chord to make the transition from chord to chord more convenient. Instead of fretting the Em chord with the second and third fingers as before, we can try the first and second fingers as shown in the diagram below. Now your first finger can stay on the same note for both chords. Starting with the G chord, simply lift your third finger from the fretboard while moving your second finger into place on the fourth string. Your first finger will probably slide backward a little to make room for your second finger.

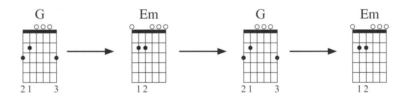

D Chord

The open D major chord is played on the four highest-pitched strings (don't strum the fifth and sixth strings).

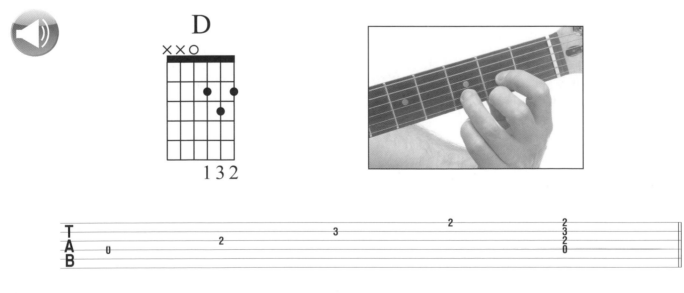

The G and D major chords are often found next to each other in chord progressions, so it's important for you to get comfortable changing from one to the other. All three fingers need to move for the transition, but once you get used to the motion, it's a fairly comfortable chord change. Notice that your first and third fingers stay at the same frets while moving to different strings. Your second finger moves in a diagonal motion (down and back) from the third fret to the second fret. Try to avoid taking your whole hand off the fretboard; make the motion as minimal as possible, lifting your fingers just slightly off the strings. Also remember that you're only strumming the fourth through first strings for the D chord.

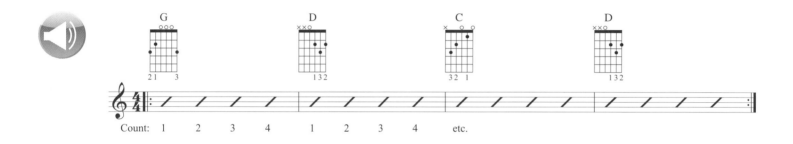

Here's an example that incorporates three chords: G, C, and D. These chords are often used together in many rock and blues songs. Practice these transitions until you can play them in time without hesitating. This example uses *repeat signs*, so play through the progression two times without stopping.

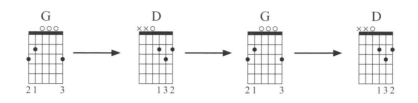

A Chord

The open A major chord is played by stacking your first three fingers at the second fret as shown below. You'll need to scrunch your fingers together to get them all to fit within the one fret. Make sure that each note is sounding out cleanly, with no fret buzz. For this particular voicing of the A major chord, the first and fifth strings are played open, so be careful not to accidentally deaden them with your fingers.

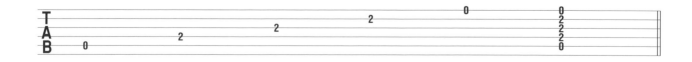

Here's an example that incorporates the A major chord with the D and E major chords. These three chords are used together in many chord progressions and songs.

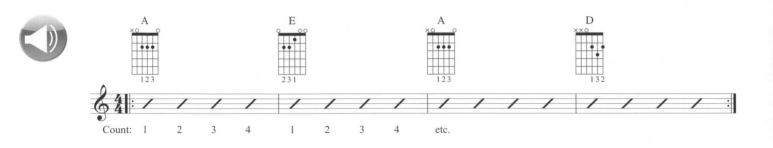

Dm Chord

Our final open chord for this chapter is the D minor chord. Similar to the D major chord, it uses three fingers to fret the chord and is also played on the highest four strings (don't strum the fifth and sixth strings).

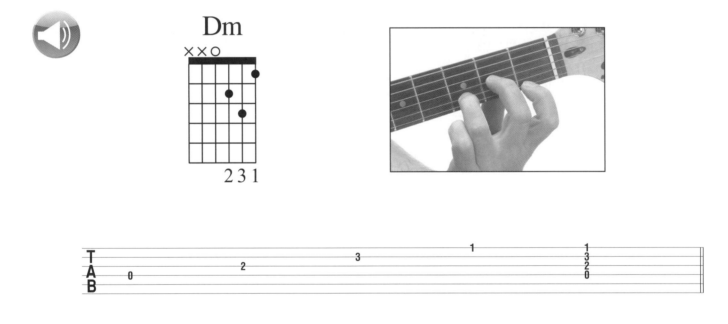

Here's a quick review of the eight chords covered in this chapter. These chords represent the most popular and commonly played chords on the guitar. In the next chapter, we'll use them in chord progressions and rhythms to get you more comfortable with changing chords and playing songs.

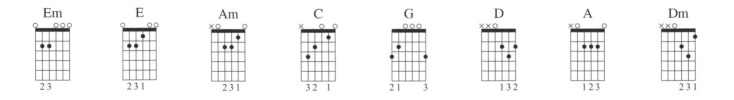

Chapter 3
Rhythm and Strumming Patterns

Along with melody and harmony, rhythm is one of the most important elements of music. Although it isn't essential for you to learn how to read musical notes at this point, it is helpful to learn how to count rhythms and play in time. In this chapter, we'll explore some basic rhythm patterns and a simple system used to notate them.

Rhythm Slashes

Rhythm guitar parts are often notated via a system of slashes (instead of traditional oval notes and pitches) that rhythmically show when the chords are strummed and how long they should be held or sustained. In 4/4 time (common time), a *quarter note* is equal to one beat, and four quarter notes make up a complete measure of music.

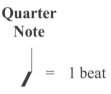

The example below shows a chord progression that's played with all downstrokes and quarter notes. Each chord should be held for the same amount of time. Don't pause or hesitate while changing chords and be sure to keep the rhythm steady.

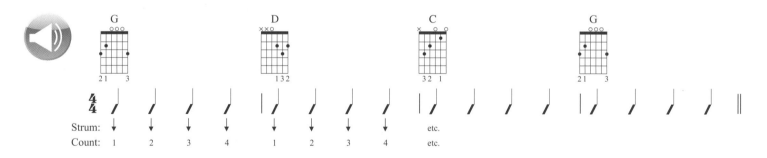

Whole notes are held for four beats, and *half notes* are held for two beats. Their slashes are indicated using open noteheads as shown below. The example that follows uses all half notes and whole notes.

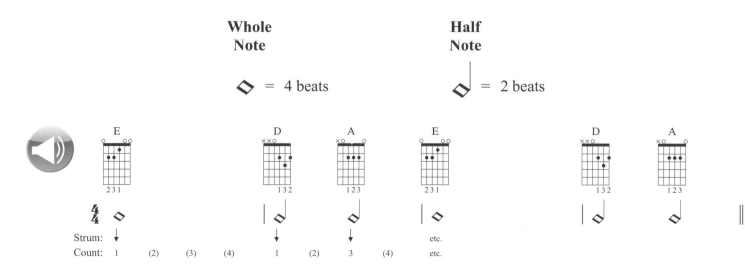

Eighth notes are held for half of a beat. A single eighth note is notated using a single flag on its stem as shown below. Multiple eighth notes are usually joined at the top with a horizontal beam instead of flags.

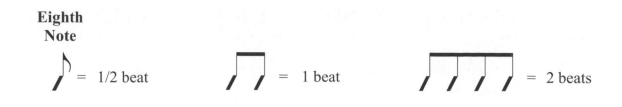

Eighth notes can be counted using "and" in-between the beats ("one-and, two-and," etc.). The example below uses steady eighth notes and *alternate strumming* throughout. The chords on beats 1, 2, 3, and 4 are called *downbeats* and are played using downstrokes. The chords that fall on "and" are called *upbeats* and are played with upstrokes. The strumming is faster than the previous quarter-note example, but be sure to keep it consistent and steady, without pausing between chords.

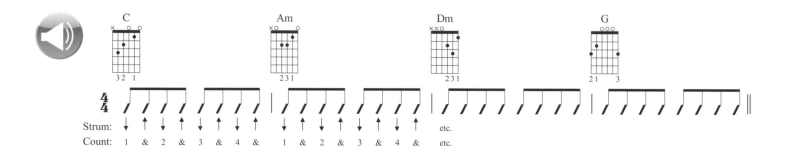

This next example is a common rhythm that combines quarter notes and eighth notes. Notice that we are still playing all of the downbeats with downstrokes, instead of using continuous alternate strumming.

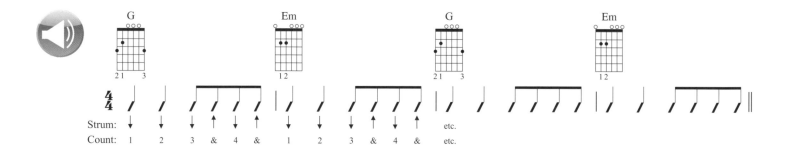

Sixteenth notes are held for one quarter of a beat. A single 16th note is notated using a double flag on its stem. Multiple 16th notes that all fall within the same beat can be grouped together using a double horizontal beam instead of flags.

Here's an example using alternate strumming and steady 16th notes. Start at a slow and even tempo and make sure that your strumming is consistent. Count "one-e-and-a, two-e-and-a," etc.

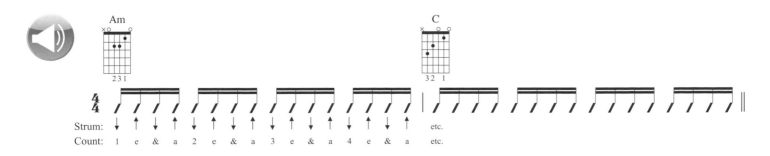

Our next example mixes eighth notes and 16th notes. The eighth notes on the downbeats use downstrums, followed by a down-up alternate strum for the 16th notes on the second half of each beat.

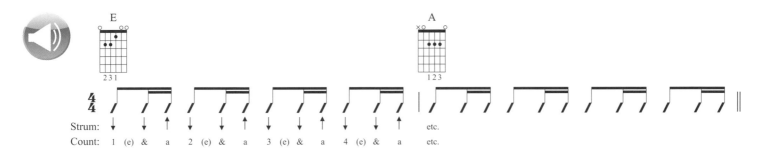

Strummin' Blues

Here's a song that incorporates some of the previous chords into a blues progression. It's common to show the chord frames (diagrams) once at the beginning of a song, in the order that they're used, then just show the chord symbols (letter names) above the rhythm slashes. The strumming pattern and count are indicated under the first measure and are consistent throughout. Notice that this example also uses repeat signs.

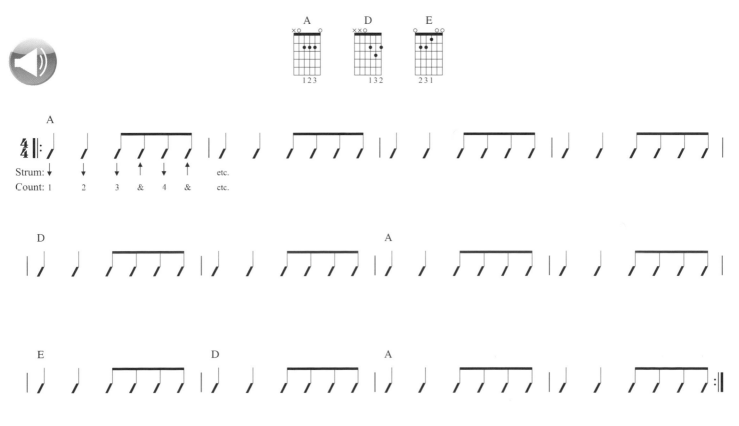

Ties and Dots

A tie is a curved line connecting two slashes of the same chord, indicating that you should only strum the first slash and let it sustain for the duration of both slashes combined. For example, two whole notes tied together indicate one strum sustained for a total of eight beats. Two eighth notes tied together would equal one beat.

A dot placed after a slash increases its duration by one half of its original value. For example, since a half note is worth two beats, placing a dot after it increases the duration by an extra beat, making it three beats total. If a dot is placed after a quarter note, it becomes one-and-a-half beats total.

Here's an example that contains some ties and dotted notes. Notice that the strumming pattern uses downstrokes on some of the upbeats where the chords change. This is to emphasize the upbeats instead of the downbeats, also known as *syncopation*.

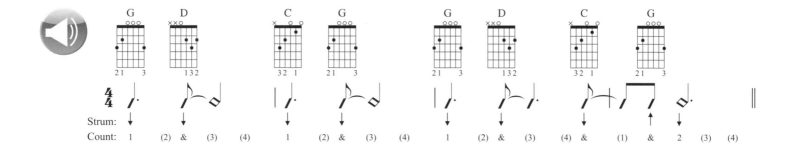

This next example incorporates a dotted eighth note/16th note figure on beat 2 of each measure. It may seem tricky at first, but once you've got a feel for how it's played, you probably won't need to count it out. Notice that we're using the alternate Em chord fingering to make switching to the G chord easier.

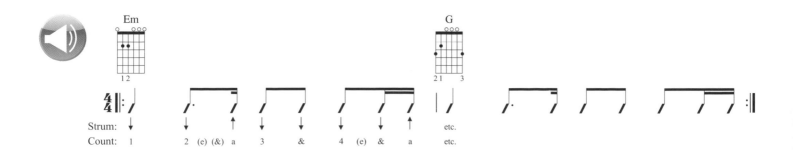

18

Rests

A rest is used to indicate silence—where no note or chord is played. Rests also have rhythmic values that tell you how long the silence should last. The universal symbols for musical rests are shown below. Dots can also be added to rests to increase their duration by one half the original value.

Whole Rest (4 beats)	Half Rest (2 beats)	Quarter Rest (1 beat)	Eighth Rest (1/2 beat)	16th Rest (1/4 beat)

Here's an example that incorporates some of the different types of rests. For each rest, make sure that you mute the previous chord and that there is complete silence during the rest. For example, in measure 2, allow the A chord to ring out for the first two beats, then mute it so that the silence begins right on beat 3.

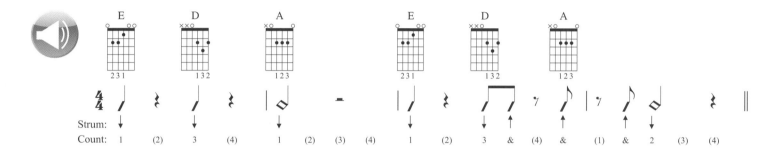

Triplets

A triplet is a group of three equivalent notes played within the space of two. The most common triplet is the eighth-note triplet, where three notes are played within one beat, dividing the beat into three equal-length notes. Eighth-note triplets are counted "one-and-a, two-and-a," etc. Triplets are indicated by using a "3" above the beamed or bracketed group of notes, as shown in the example below.

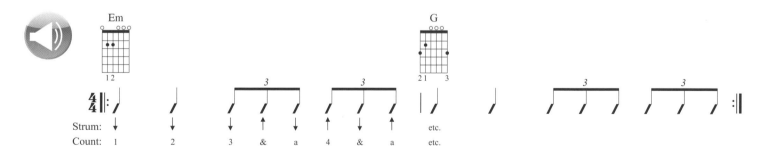

Triplets can be any combination of notes and rests of equivalent value, and can also contain notes that are further subdivided within the triplet. Any grouping of notes that add up to three within the space of two are considered triplets. The notation for half-note, quarter-note, and 16th-note triplet groups are shown below.

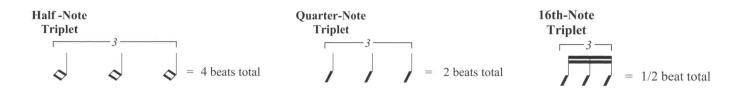

Rockin' Blues

Here's another song that uses a variation of the standard blues progression, this time in the key of G. The strumming pattern uses eighth notes and ties, and the count is indicated under the first measure.

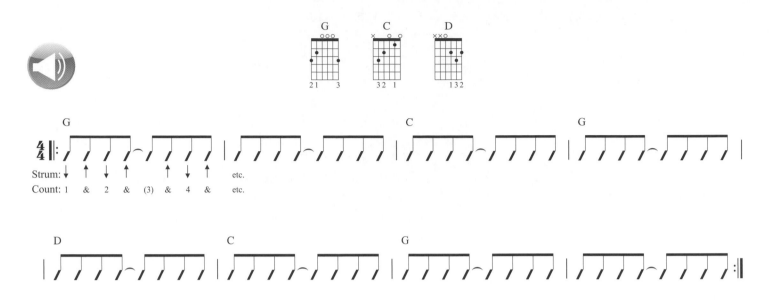

Review

The following chart summarizes some of the various slash and rest symbols used throughout this book.

NAME OF NOTE	RHYTHM SLASHES	REST SYMBOLS	COUNTS (AND NUMBER OF BEATS)
Whole Note	◊	▬	1 (2) (3) (4)
Half Note	◊	▬	1 (2) 3 (4)
Quarter Note	/	𝄽	1 2 3 4
Eighth Note	♪ ♫	𝄾	1 & 2 & 3 & 4 &
16th Note	♬	𝄿	1 e & a 2 e & a 3 e & a 4 e & a
Eighth-Note Triplet	3		3 3 3 3 \n 1 & a 2 & a 3 & a 4 & a

Chapter 4
Closed-position Major and Minor Chords

Once you've mastered all of the chords from Chapter 2, there's just a few more left to learn so that you can play all of the regular major and minor chords in the first area of the fretboard. The chords in this chapter are *closed-position* chords because they contain no open strings. There are numerous ways to play any chord on the guitar, but the versions presented in this chapter are the easiest ones to get you started. We'll explore different ways to play all of the chords in upcoming chapters.

F Chord

The most basic version of the F major chord is played on the four highest-pitched strings. It contains what's called a *barre* (pronounced "bar"), which is a technique used to fret multiple strings with one finger. This technique can be challenging for beginners, but you should practice it until you've got it mastered because the barre is essential for playing many other chords.

In the following chord diagram, the curved line on top connecting the dots represents a barre. Lay your first finger flat across the first and second strings at the first fret, pressing down on both strings simultaneously. Pick each note to make sure that you're applying enough pressure to produce clean pitches. Now comes the hard part—adding the notes at the second and third frets. Your second and third fingers need to be arched as usual to properly fret those notes, while keeping your first finger laid flat and holding the barre. You will probably need to angle your hand slightly, and your first finger will naturally shift slightly so that you're actually pressing down with the outside edge of the first joint, not the spongy part of the finger. Although it may feel uncomfortable at first (like you're pressing the string down with your bone), this is natural and it should become easier with a little practice. As before, pick each note of the chord individually to make sure that all pitches sound clean, not muted or buzzing.

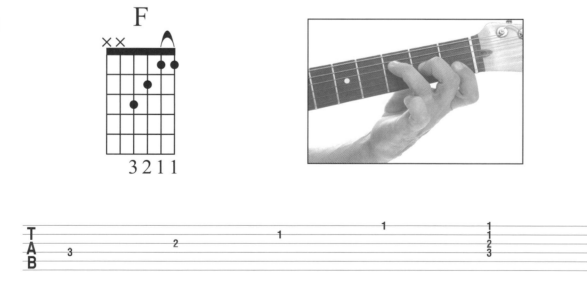

The next exercise is a rhythm example in slashes that switches from the F to the Dm chord. This is a common chord change that you should get familiar with since these two chords are often found together in chord progressions. You might find it easier to keep the barre held throughout both chords so that the only finger that needs to move is your third finger.

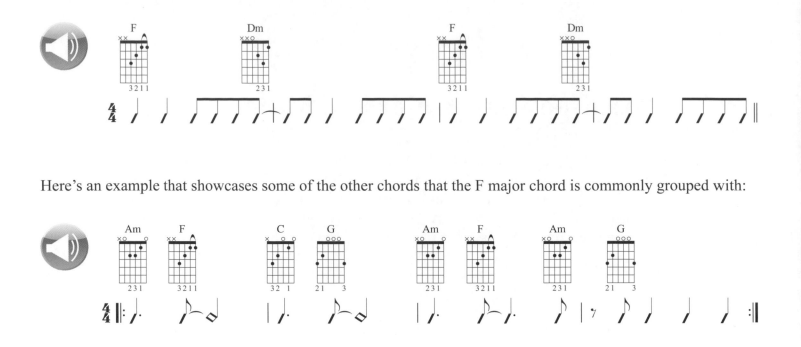

Here's an example that showcases some of the other chords that the F major chord is commonly grouped with:

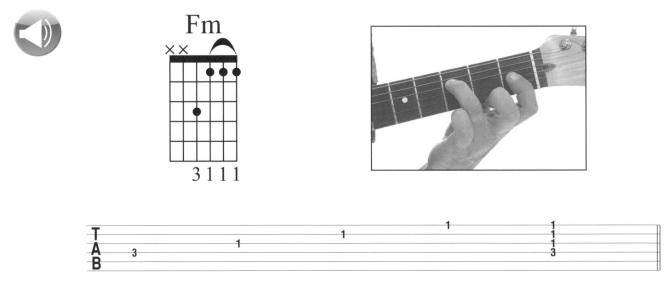

Fm and Gm Chords

Fm is similar to the F major chord; however, you need to barre your first finger across three strings instead of two. Pick each note individually before strumming to make sure that you're applying enough even pressure to the barre, and that you're arching your third finger properly while stretching it up to the third fret.

Since these chords are closed-position chords and contain no open strings, you can move (*transpose*) them to other keys. Simply move the entire Fm chord two frets higher, and it becomes a Gm chord.

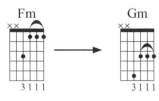

B Chord

Here's a basic version of the B major chord that's played on the four highest strings and doesn't use a barre. Notice how the second, third, and fourth fingers are stacked at the same fret, similar to the open A major chord. The challenge with this fingering is the stretch that's required to reach back to the second fret with your first finger.

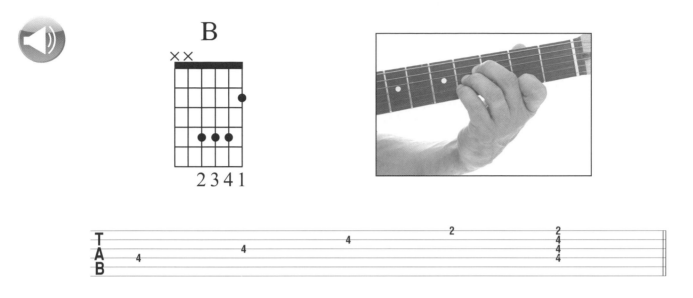

Bm and Cm Chords

Here's a commonly used version of the closed-position Bm chord. Stack your third and fourth fingers at the fourth fret, covering the third and fourth strings, respectively. From there, your second and first fingers should easily be able to reach the other two notes in the chord.

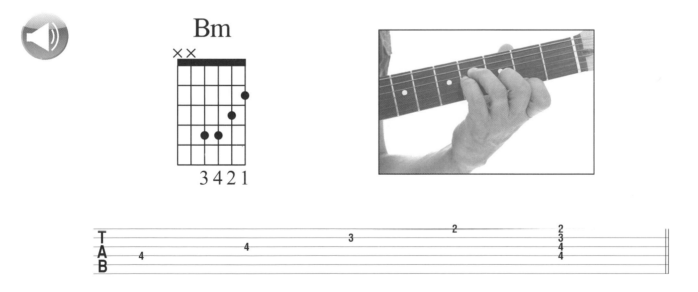

We can also transpose the Bm chord to Cm by moving it up one fret.

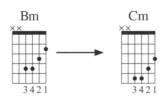

Jammin' Reggae

Here's an example that mixes some of the closed-position major and minor chords. Reggae-style guitar rhythms often emphasize beats 2 and 4, and rest on beats 1 and 3. Use upstrokes for all of the chords.

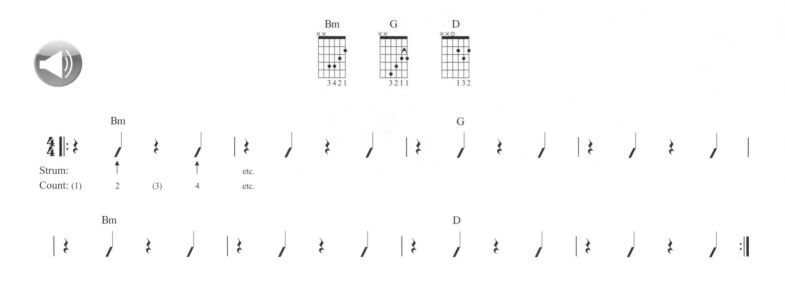

The Rising Sun

This example uses some of the chords from the previous sections for a song in 6/8 time—six eighth notes per measure. 6/8 is played with a triplet feel (groups of threes), placing the emphasis on beats 1 and 4, counted as **one**-two-three, **four**-five-six. The rhythm is strummed using downstrokes, except for the down-up strummed 16th notes in each measure. Play in a steady and even tempo, and make sure that you've got the chord changes sounding clean, with no pauses in-between.

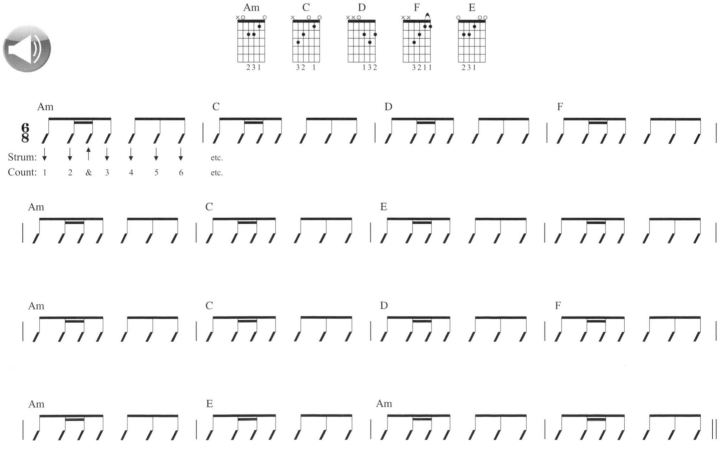

Chapter 5
Power Chords

Regular major and minor chords on the guitar are comprised of three different notes: the root (the note that gives the chord its letter name), the 3rd (the third note in the scale above the root note), and the 5th (the fifth note in the scale above the root note). Guitar chords consist of a configuration of these notes within one position on the fretboard. For example, the three different notes in a C major chord are C, E, and G—the first (root), third, and fifth notes of the C major scale (**C**–D–**E**–F–**G**–A–B–C). The root and 5th are the same distance apart (in pitch) for both the major and minor chords; however, the 3rd is lower in a minor chord than it is in a major chord, and this is what distinguishes major from minor.

If we leave out the 3rd and just play a simple two-note chord comprised of the root and 5th, this will give us a *power chord* that is neither major nor minor. Power chords are used extensively in hard rock and metal, and they sound great on an electric guitar with distortion. They are mostly played on the lower-sounding strings. Power chords are indicated with a "5" in the chord name; for example, E5.

Sixth-string Power Chords

Power chords are easy to play and require just the first and third fingers to fret the notes. They are also movable chords that can be transposed and played at any fret. Here are some of the commonly played sixth-string power chords, including the open E5 power chord:

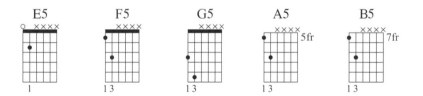

Here's an example that uses some of the sixth-string power chords. Power chords generally sound better played with all downstrokes. Make sure that you're only strumming the lowest two strings.

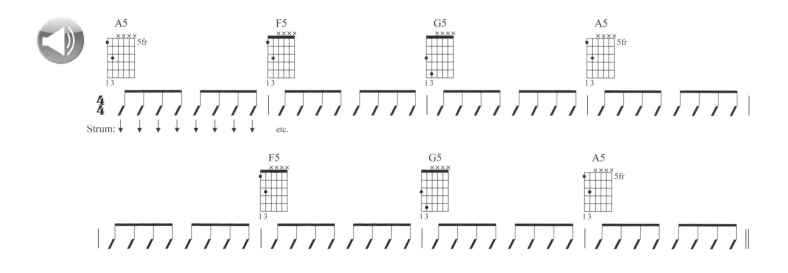

Since power chords can be played anywhere on the fretboard, it's helpful to learn and memorize some of the notes on the neck. Learning a little bit about the musical alphabet will make this easier. The musical alphabet uses the letters A through G. The distance in pitch between any two notes is called an *interval*. An interval is how much higher or lower one note sounds from another (or the space between the two notes). The smallest interval on a guitar is the distance from one fretted note to the next fretted note on the same string. This interval is called a *half step*. Twice that distance, or the distance of two frets on the same string, is called a *whole step*. Below are the regular letter-name notes on the sixth string, with the half steps and whole steps indicated.

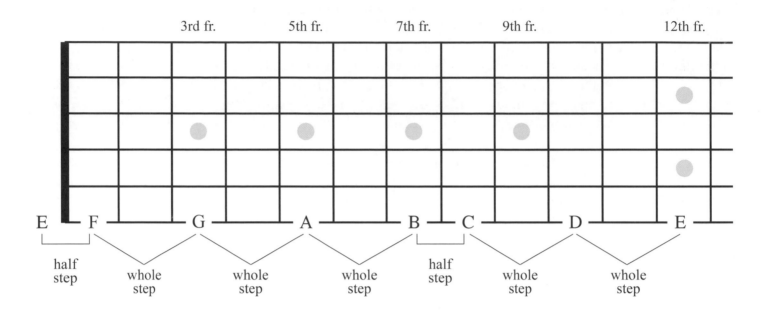

The regular letter-name notes shown above are called *natural notes*. This formula of half steps and whole steps are a consistent characteristic in all music; half steps exist naturally between the notes B and C, and the notes E and F. Whole steps exist between all of the other natural notes. The notes that fall in between the natural whole steps are *sharps* (♯) or *flats* (♭). A sharp placed on a note raises its pitch by a half step; a flat placed on a note lowers its pitch by a half step. For example, the note between A and B can either be called A♯ or B♭ (depending on the key and context of the music). Below is a diagram that shows all of the notes on the sixth string, including the sharp and flat notes, from the low open E to the next higher E at the 12th fret.

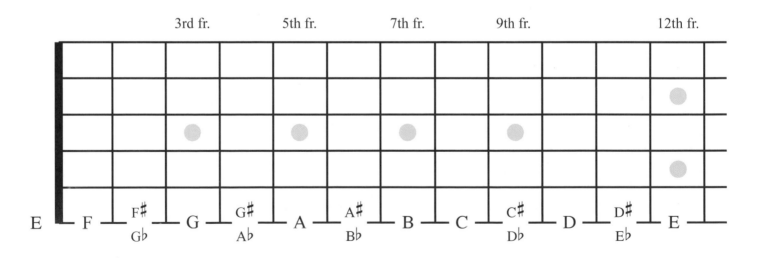

The interval (distance) from the open E to the higher E at the 12th fret is called an *octave*. After the 12th fret, the musical alphabet repeats (the note at the 13th fret is F, the note at the 14th fret is F♯, and so on).

Fifth-string Power Chords

Here are some of the commonly played fifth-string power chords, including the open A5 power chord:

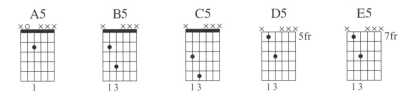

This next example uses some of the fifth-string power chords in a typical metal-style rhythm. Use all downstrokes and be sure that you're not accidentally hitting any of the other strings and causing unwanted string noise, especially if you're playing an electric guitar with distortion.

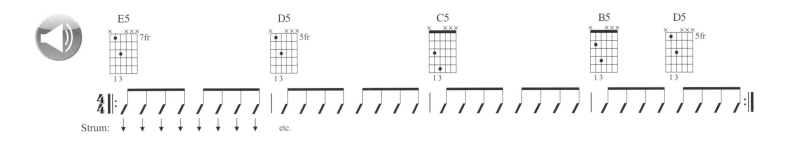

Here's a chart that shows all of the notes on the fifth string so that you can play the fifth-string power chord at any fret. Notice that the half step/whole step rules apply here, too—that is, the natural half steps occur between B and C, and between E and F.

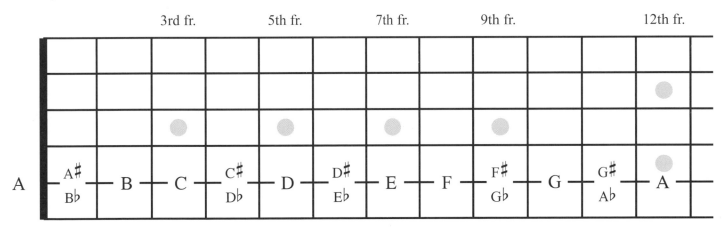

The following example mixes the fifth- and sixth-string power chords in a rhythm that's reminiscent of "Rock You Like a Hurricane" by the Scorpions.

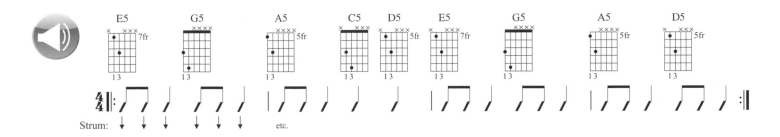

27

Chords in Tab and the Shuffle Rhythm

Oftentimes rhythm guitar parts will be notated in tab instead of slashes, especially in the case of power chords or rhythm parts that incorporate some single notes or riffs. The rhythm can be shown in tablature using the same system of stems and beams that are used for slashes.

This next example is a common rock and blues pattern that alternates the E5 chord with an E6 chord. We've provided the frames so that you can see the left-hand fingering. You'll need to stretch your fourth finger five frets to reach the 11th fret, but this is a very common chord change and you should get comfortable with it. The example is played in a straight eighth-note rhythm, written in tab with stems and beams.

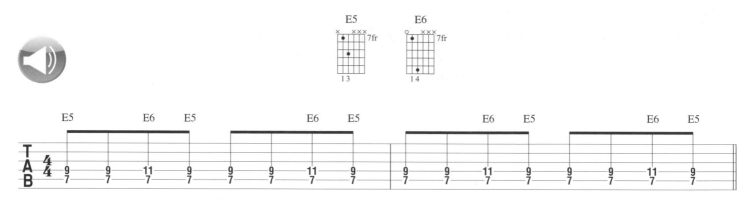

Many rock and blues songs are played with a *shuffle feel*. In a shuffle feel, the second eighth note of each beat lags a little. It's much easier to get a grasp of what shuffle feel should sound like by listening to it, and you can hear it used in many blues standards. Technically, it's the same as dividing each beat into a triplet, but only playing the first and third notes of the triplet, as shown below.

Instead of showing music in a shuffle feel using triplets, it will almost always be written out as regular eighth notes, but with an equivalency indicated at the beginning of the song, in parentheses above the time signature. This tells you that the eighths should be played in a shuffle feel. The example below uses the shuffle feel and the fifth- and sixth-string power chords in open position. Use your first and third fingers to fret the notes at the second and fourth frets, respectively. You'll probably recognize this example as one of the most commonly played blues progressions.

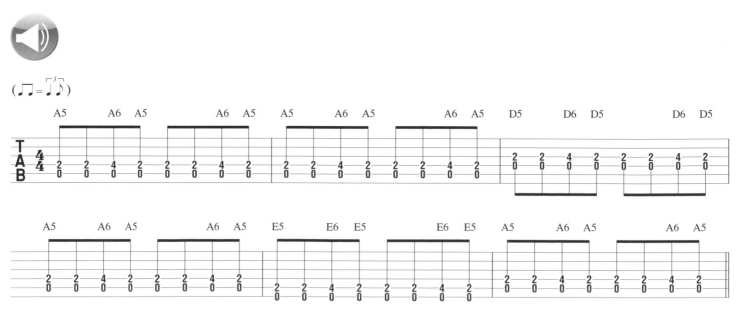

Chapter 6
Suspensions and Alterations

You can beef up your rhythm playing and have fun with the open chords by adding some simple suspensions. The most common suspension is the suspended 4th (sus4), which creates tension by substituting the 3rd of the chord with the 4th. Suspended chords are often followed by the regular major chord, creating what's known as a *suspension and resolution*. One of the most common chord suspensions is the open Dsus4 chord. Starting with the open D chord, just keep your second finger in place on the first string while adding your fourth finger to the third fret to perform the suspension.

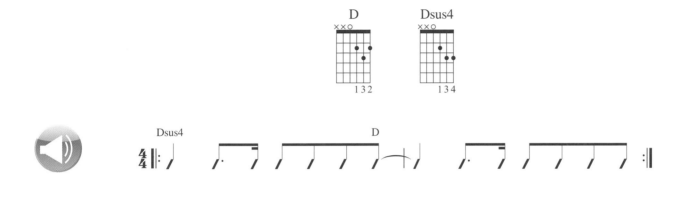

Here's an example using the Dsus4 chord in a shuffle feel. This rhythm part is reminiscent of many songs, and can be heard during the intro to "Crazy Little Thing Called Love" by Queen.

The suspended 2nd (sus2) chord is similar to the sus4 chord, except the 3rd of the chord is substituted with the 2nd. To play the Dsus2 chord, start with the D major chord and simply lift your second finger from the first string and play it open. The example below combines the D major, Dsus2, and Dsus4 chords in a simple rhythm.

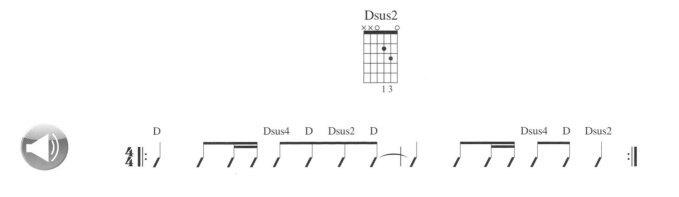

The open Esus4 chord can be played by starting with a regular E major chord and then just adding your fourth finger to the second fret of the third string. To play the rhythm below, keep your first finger in place at the first fret for the E chord, and switch between adding and removing the fourth finger at the second fret. This rhythm is similar to "She Talks to Angels" by the Black Crowes.

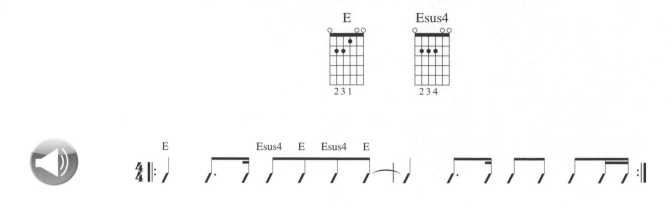

A suspended 4th can also be added to the F major chord by using your fourth finger at the third fret while keeping the rest of the F major chord fretted. See how easy it is to create interesting rhythm parts with suspensions? You should be getting the hang of these by now.

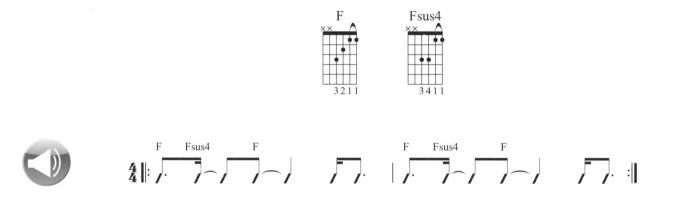

Here are the sus2 and sus4 chords that can be used with the open A major chord. Keep in mind that suspensions don't always need to resolve. While the sus4 has a real tendency to want to resolve to major, the sus2 chord can be used very effectively on its own, creating a wide-open-sounding chord that's neither major nor minor.

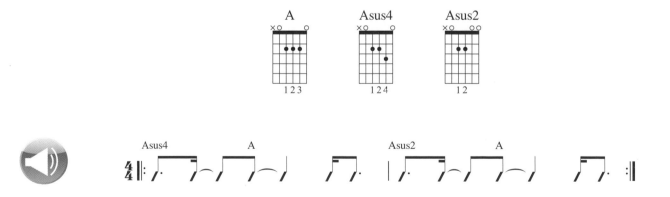

Here's a popular example centered around a C major chord and a Cadd2 chord. The add2 chord here is functioning much like a sus2 chord; however, since the 3rd of the chord is still present (the high open E string is the 3rd of a C major chord), technically it isn't a pure sus2. Hence the "add2" name, because we're actually adding a 2nd to the full C major chord instead of suspending it. Starting with the C chord, simply lift your second finger from the fourth string and play it open to get the Cadd2.

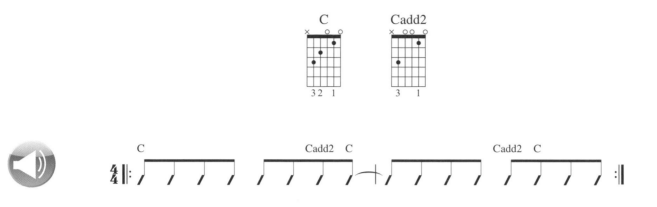

Some great progressions can be created in the key of G by slightly altering the voicing or fingering of the open G major chord. Below is a variation of the traditional G major chord, this time fretted with all four fingers. By moving the first and second fingers downward one string (and leaving the third and fourth fingers stationary), you'll get what's called a Cadd9 chord. This progression has been used extensively in many styles of music, and is similar to the beginning of "I'll Remember You" by Skid Row.

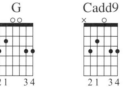

Here's a variation of the previous example. The rhythm is the same, but by removing the 3rd from each chord, the chord names change to G5 and Csus2. Notice that the chord fingerings are basically the same as before, except you're leaving out the first finger. Instead, angle your second finger downward a little so that it slightly touches and effectively deadens the adjacent string, muting the fifth string for the G5 chord, and the fourth string for the Csus2 chord.

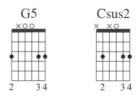

Let's take the G5 chord from the previous example and create a G5–G6 progression. Simply add your first finger to the second fret of the fourth string to fret the G6 chord. In this case, the 6th sounds something like a suspension and can be used sparingly for progressions in G.

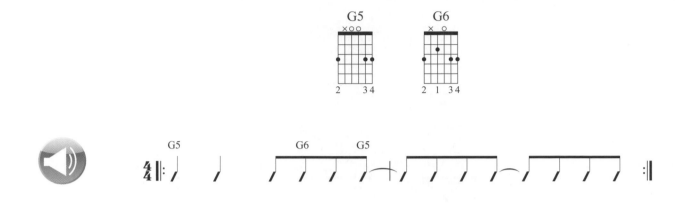

Here's another variation on the G–Cadd9 progression. This time we'll fret both chords with just two fingers, effectively changing the chord names to G and Cmaj7. Notice that you just need to move your second finger by one string and you've got it. We'll explore many of the other seventh chords in the next chapter.

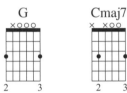

If we take the above version of the open G major chord and change the fingering so as to fret it with the third and fourth fingers, it opens up many other possibilities for suspensions and alteration. As before, angle your third finger downward slightly to mute the fifth string. By adding your second finger to the second fret of the third string, you'll create a Gadd9 chord. Similarly, by adding your first finger to the first fret of the second string, you'll be playing a Gsus4 chord.

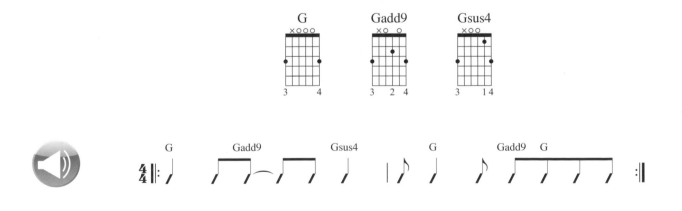

Let's stick with the previous open G chord fingering, then combine the suspended 4th and the 6th at the same time. This configuration of notes actually spells out a full C major chord, but the note G remains as the lowest-sounding note. This is known as a C chord with G in the bass, indicated by the slashed chord name, C/G.

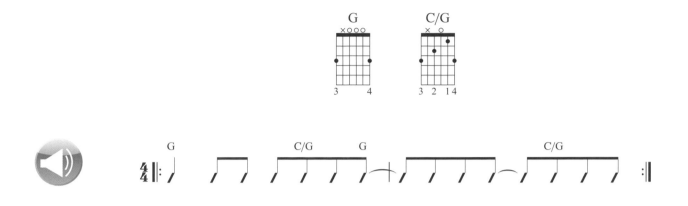

Suspended 4ths and 2nds are commonly used with major chords, but they can also be effective sometimes with minor chords. Here's a progression in A minor that employs an Asus2 and Asus4 chord. The second measure uses the same G–Gsus4 progression from a few examples back.

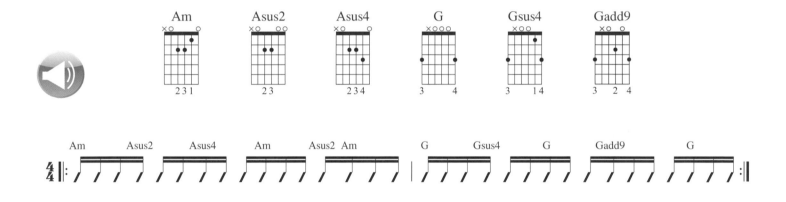

By *inverting* a chord (using a different bass note), you can create smooth transitions within chord progressions. This next example features two popular moves used to connect from C to Am, and from G to Em. Take notice of which strings to mute and strum for the G/B and G/F♯ chords in order to avoid playing unwanted notes.

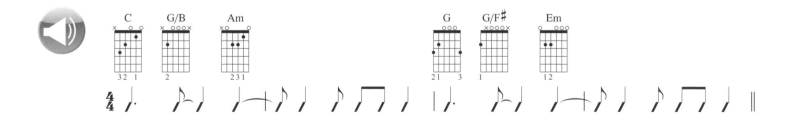

Here's a variation of the previous example shown in tablature and using single notes to pick out (or *arpeggiate*) some of the chords. In the third measure, the notes of the second chord spell out a perfect D/F♯. Let the notes ring out over each other for the arpeggiated chords.

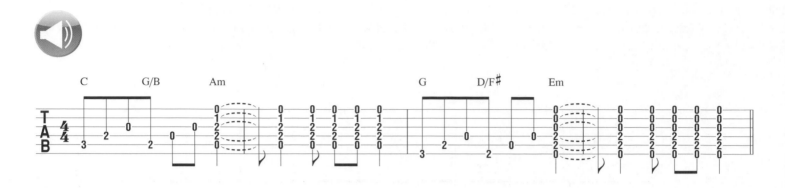

Here's a common variation of the open A major chord fingering, played by barring the three fretted notes with one finger. Notice that the first string is muted. You can accomplish this by slightly angling the second joint of your finger outward to deaden the string, or by being precise with your strumming so that you only strum strings 5–2.

The open A barre is useful when creating riffs in A that combine the chord with single notes, riffs, and inversions, as shown in the following examples. In the chord analysis above the tab staff, "N.C." stands for "no chord" and is usually used to indicate single notes.

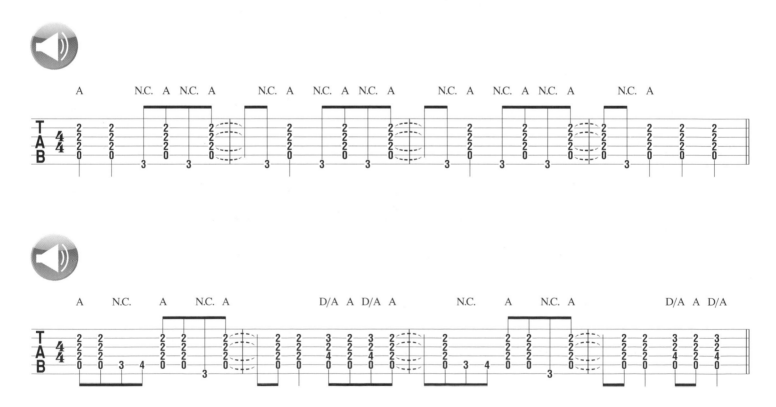

Chapter 7
Open Seventh Chords

In earlier chapters, we showed how major and minor chords are comprised of the root, third and fifth steps of the scale. By continuing this pattern of using every odd numbered interval above the root note, we can add the next chord tone, the 7th. The three most popular seventh chords are the *dominant seventh* (7), the *major seventh* (maj7), and the *minor seventh* (m7). Each of the seventh chords has a formula of intervals that combine to create its unique sound and tonal quality. In this chapter, we'll focus on the most commonly used open seventh chords.

Dominant Seventh Chords

Dominant seventh chords (also known simply as "seventh chords") have a major 3rd and a flat (minor) 7th, giving them a distinct bluesy sound. Here are some of the common open seventh chords:

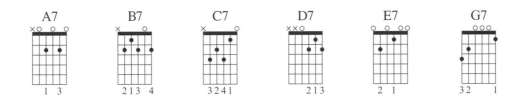

The next two examples use the above dominant seventh chords in traditional blues progressions. The first example is a slow blues shuffle in the key of G, using the G7, C7, and D7 fingerings. The second example is a straight rock feel in the key of A, using the A7, D7, and E7 chord fingerings.

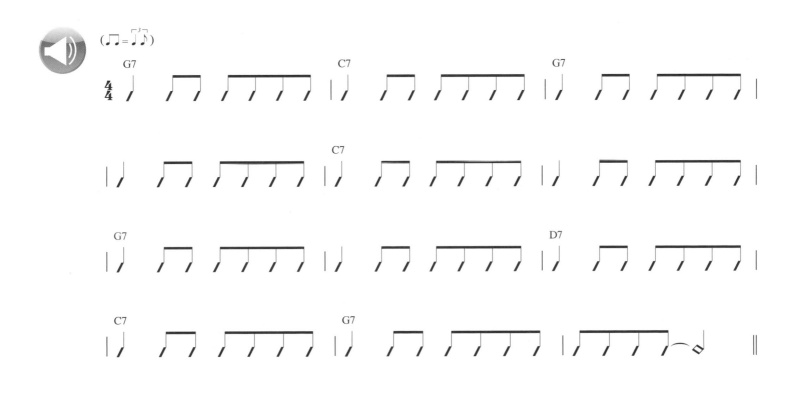

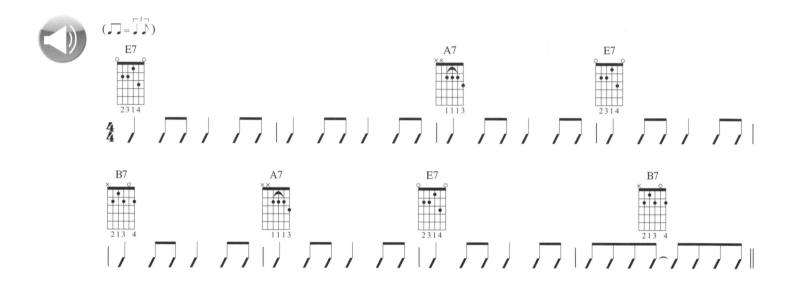

This next example is a blues shuffle that showcases alternate fingerings for the E7 and A7 chords. Depending on the context within a progression or song, these fingerings might be preferable. Notice that we've used a barre to play the A7 chord, but you can also try fretting the notes with individual fingers instead. Experiment with the different fingerings and decide for yourself which versions work best for you.

Major Seventh Chords

Major seventh chords contain a major 3rd and a major 7th. They have a light, jazzy quality, and may remind you of happiness, sunshine, and summertime. Here are some popular fingerings for the open major seventh chords:

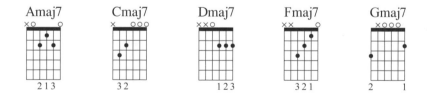

The following major seventh chord example combines the Cmaj7 chord with an Em chord, and is reminiscent of the intro to David Bowie's "Space Oddity." Notice that the Em chord uses the first and second fingers to fret the notes, making the chord change easy. Simply leave your second finger in place for both chords and alternate between your first and third fingers on the fifth string.

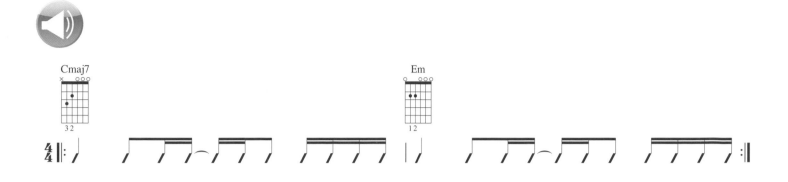

Here's an example that combines the Amaj7 and Dmaj7 chords. We've substituted the original Dmaj7 fingering with a first-finger barre. As with the previous examples, try both fingerings to see which one works for you. Throughout this book, we've presented various fingerings for many of the chords to show you that chord fingerings and voicings don't need to follow rigid rules, and once you're aware of the notes in the chord, you can choose to adjust the fingering to suit the context.

This next example is a D–Gmaj7 progression in 6/8 time. We've altered the Gmaj7 fingering here so that the chord is played with your second and third fingers. In this case, you can leave your second finger stationary for both chords. To switch to the Gmaj7, simply lift your first finger and move your third finger from the second string to the sixth string.

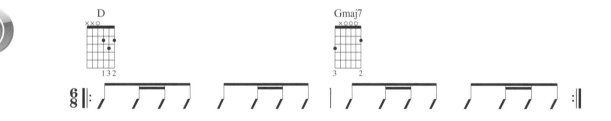

Here's a common use of the Fmaj7 chord in a progression. Notice how easy it is to switch from Fmaj7 to C—just leave your first finger in place and move your second and third fingers to the fourth and fifth strings, respectively.

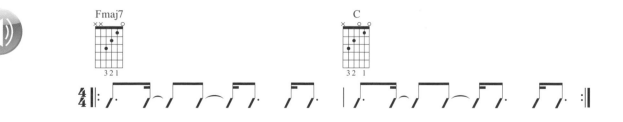

Now let's try a popular variation of the previous example. By putting the 5th in the bass for the Fmaj7 chord, we get an Fmaj7/C inversion. To switch to the C chord, lift your fourth finger while simultaneously moving your second finger to the fourth string.

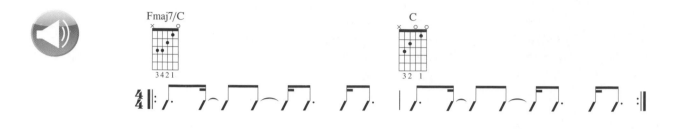

Minor Seventh Chords

Adding a minor (flatted) 7th on top of a minor chord gives us the minor seventh chords. These are darker chords, with a bit more dissonance due to the added seventh. Most minor seventh chords are easier to play in a closed position, but here are some simple open-position ones:

Am7   Dm7   Em7

The Am7 chord has most of its notes in common with the open C major chord. Here's a progression that uses those two chords, plus Dm7 and F major:

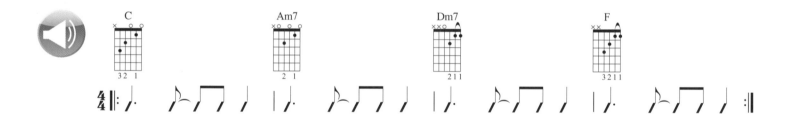

This next tablature example shows a popular way in which the Am7 chord can be combined with some single-note fills in a song. The music starts with a single-note fill on beat 4. This is called a *pickup*, a partial measure used prior to beat 1 to kick off the progression.

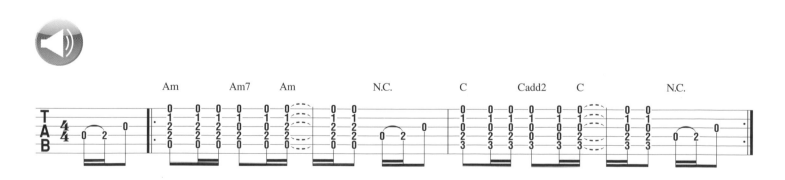

Here's an example that uses the Em7 chord, along with the traditional G major chord from Chapter 2:

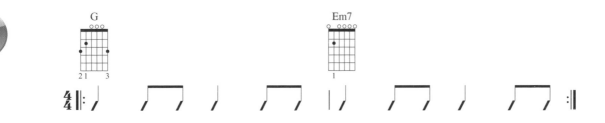

The above chord change is probably the easiest one to play in this book, but it's also not very interesting. We've already explored many variations for the open G major chord in the previous chapter, and there are just as many variations for the open Em7 chord, as well. Take a look at the following two sets of chord frames and try playing the above rhythm example by substituting these fingerings instead.

Let's take the second set of frames from above and expand on this idea. By leaving your third and fourth fingers stationary, you can come up with a pretty complex progression that's easy to play. You've probably noticed by now that the guitar lends itself to this very well. Having all of these notes in common throughout a progression will create smooth and interesting chord transitions.

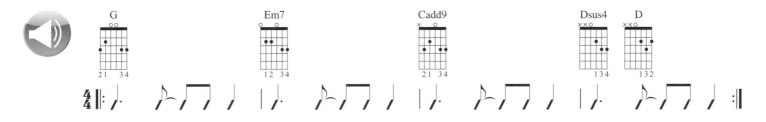

A Minor Song

The following song example, in the key of A minor, uses many of the open major, minor, and dominant seventh chords, along with some popular suspensions and alterations.

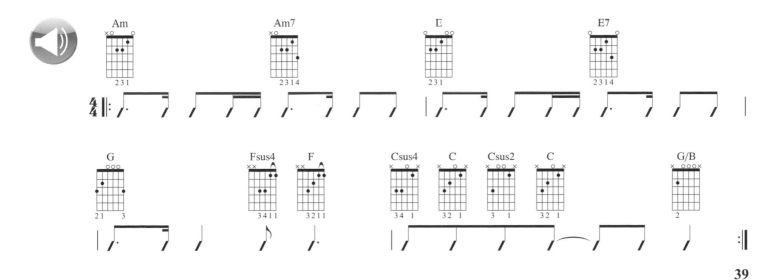

Chapter 8
Barre Chords

Learning the major and minor barre chords is an essential step toward mastering the guitar. Once you've got them down, you'll be able to play in any key on the guitar. We've used barres that covered a few strings at a time in previous chapters, but the full barre chords are especially challenging because they require you to barre across most—if not all—of the strings. Getting comfortable with this stretch may take some time, but once you've got it, you'll feel like you've truly made a breakthrough and taken your playing to the next level.

F and Fm Barre Chords

The F major barre chord is actually an extension of the closed-position F major chord that you learned in Chapter 4; we've just added the lower notes on the fifth and sixth strings. The hardest part of playing this chord is stretching your second, third, and fourth fingers out to fret the other notes while holding the barre. When played at the first fret, this major barre chord has the root note F on the sixth string. Like the power chords from Chapter 5, it can be moved up the neck and transposed. If you're having a tough time getting it to sound clean at the first fret, try moving it to the fifth or seventh fret, where the frets are closer together, until you get used to it.

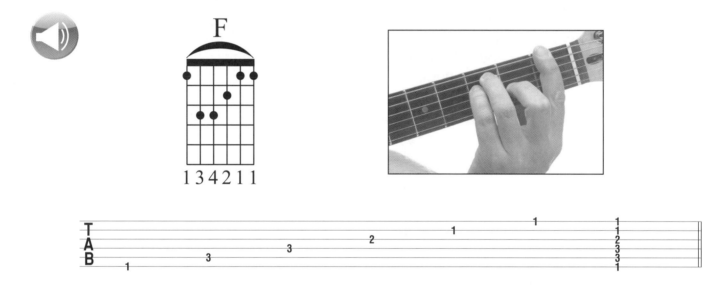

To play the Fm barre chord, simply remove your middle finger from the major barre chord and you've got it.

It's helpful to visualize the barre chords as if your first finger is acting like a movable nut. Notice that the other three fretted notes in the major barre chord are the same configuration as the open E major chord, and the additional two fretted notes in the minor barre chord are the same configuration as the open E minor chord. When you're playing these barre chords, you're essentially turning the open E major and E minor chords into closed-position chords and transposing them to different frets. You can refer to the sixth-string chart in Chapter 5 to see the name of the root note at each fret.

Here are a couple of examples that mix the sixth-string major and minor barre chords. Take your time and be sure that you're holding the barre down firmly so that all of the notes are sounding clear.

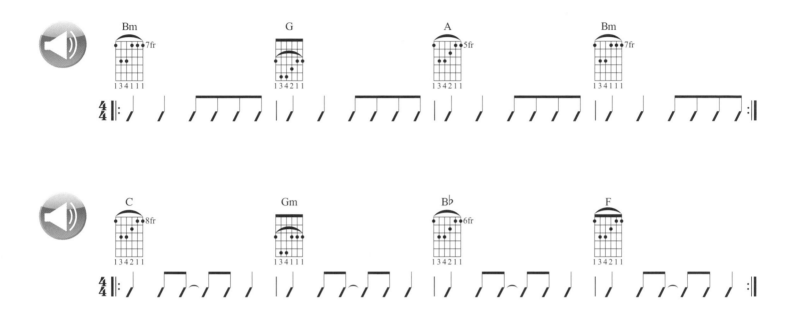

B♭ and B♭m Barre Chords

Barre chords can also be formed above root notes on the 5th string. The B♭ major barre chord at the first fret uses your third finger to barre across three strings. The first and sixth strings are muted and not strummed. Compare this chord to the open A major chord with the second, third, and fourth strings barred. Here, your first finger acts as the movable nut, fretting the root note on the fifth string.

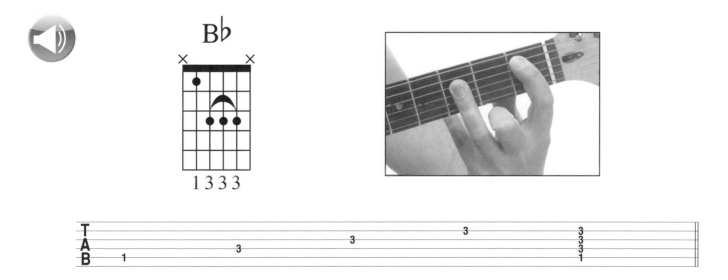

For the Bb minor barre chord, use a first-finger barre to cover the notes on the first and fifth strings. Your second, third, and fourth fingers will reach up to cover the other notes. Only the sixth string is left out and not strummed.

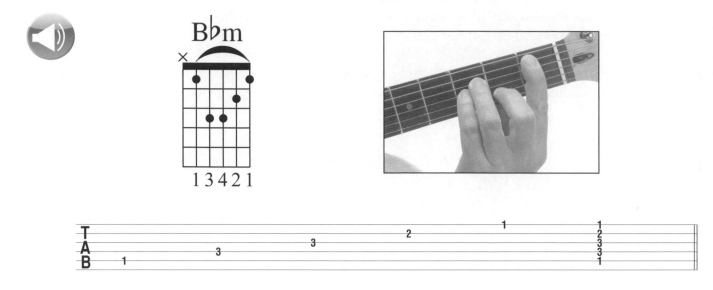

This next example demonstrates some fifth-string major and minor barre chords. Notice the muted strums just before each chord transition. This is a common practice that allows you to get your hand to the next chord while keeping the rhythm moving.

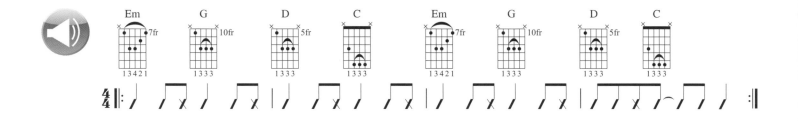

The Barre Chord Spirit Song

Here's a song that mixes all of the major and minor barre chord shapes. Start by practicing the rhythm slowly, using the alternate strumming techniques from Chapter 3 to get a consistent strumming pattern that you're comfortable with.

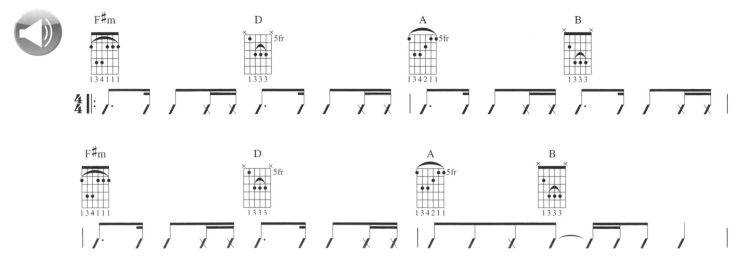

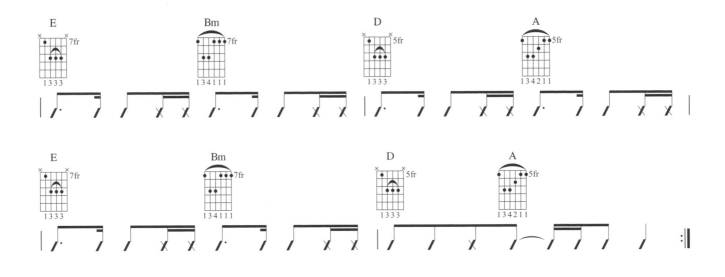

Barred Seventh Chords

By making some slight alterations to the major and minor barre chord shapes, we can add the 7ths and play closed-position major seventh, minor seventh, and dominant seventh chords. As before, there are a few popular versions. Some require a barre and some do not, but they're all movable chords and can be transposed to any fret. You can refer to the charts from Chapter 5 again, but at this point, you should be pretty familiar with the note names on the fifth and sixth strings.

Here are some of the popular fingerings for the barred seventh chords, all shown here at the fifth fret. Pay close attention to which strings are muted or not strummed.

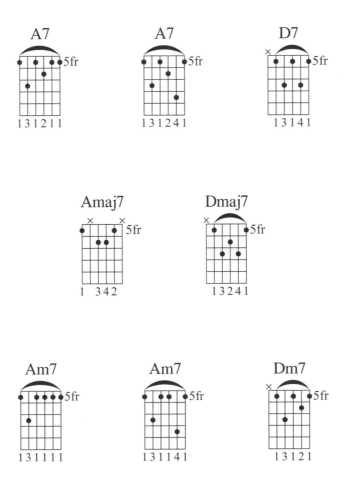

Here's a progression that showcases some of the previous closed-position seventh chords:

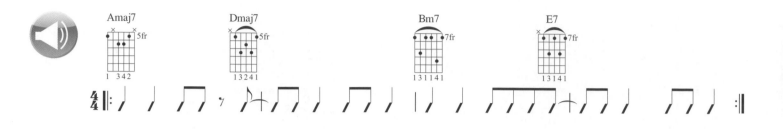

The following minor-seventh chord diagrams show a jazzier form of the minor seventh that's easy to play and sounds great. You might find this one preferable for many settings. Notice that the third finger barres most of the strings, while your second finger plays the root note on the sixth string. Slightly angle your second finger in order to deaden the fifth string. The music example, in A minor, makes good use of these chords.

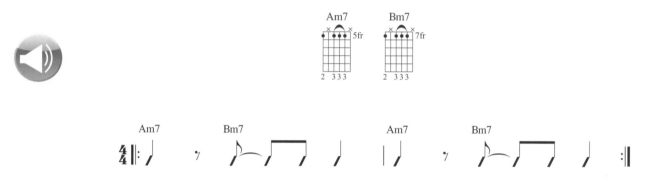

The Magic Seventh Song

Here's a song example that's a variation of the traditional blues progression, played here in the key of D minor. It uses some of the barred seventh chords covered earlier.

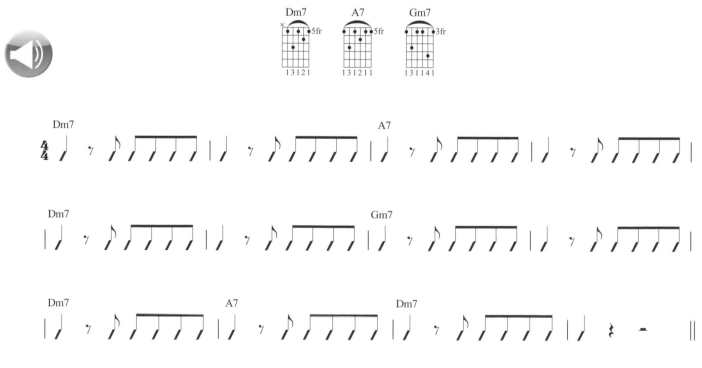

Chapter 9
Advanced Techniques

Now that we've covered most of the traditional chords used to play rhythm guitar, it's time to have some fun and break the rules. Guitarists are constantly pushing the boundaries and finding new ways to extend the range of the instrument, so you're encouraged to explore. There are basic things you can do, like put the guitar into a different or open tuning, but many artists have taken more extreme measures to smash the mold. Bands like Soundgarden have used many unique tunings on the instrument. The band Presidents of the United States played with only three strings on the guitar. Even guitarists like Jack White have replaced the low string with an actual bass string. The possibilities are endless. In this chapter, we'll give you a few of the more popular ideas to experiment with.

Moving the Open Chords

If you take the traditional open-chord shapes and move them to other frets, you'll end up with a transposed chord combined with open strings. This is a simple move that you can use to create some pretty complex chord harmonies, and with some experimentation, you'll hear which frets they sound best at. In the following examples, we've moved the open E, G, and D chords to different frets to create interesting progressions.

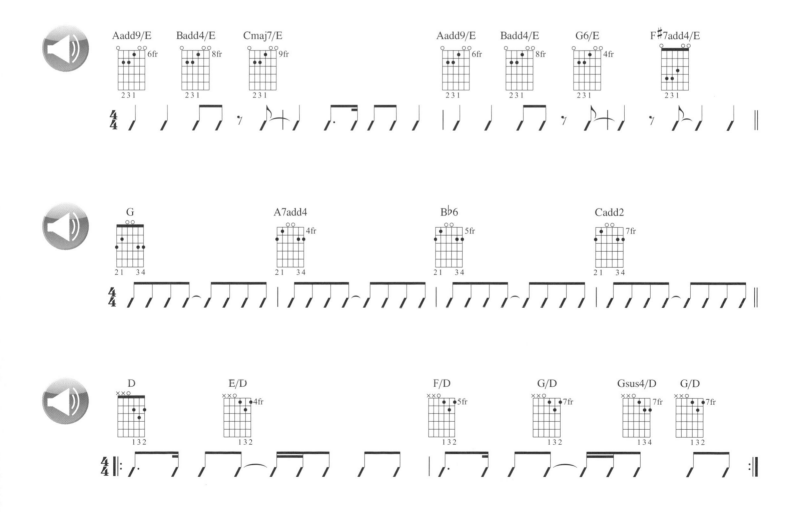

Now let's take the sixth-string major barre chord shape, but instead of barring the strings, leave the first and second strings open. These higher open strings will add interesting harmonic tones to the chords.

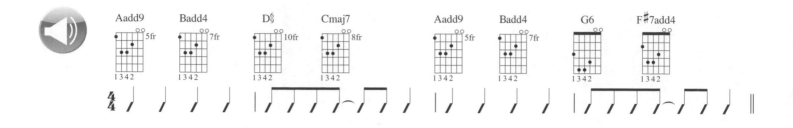

Similarly, take the fifth-string major barre chord, but only fret the lower three notes, using your first, third, and fourth fingers. The chord shape is like a power chord, with an octave added on top. Leave the first and second strings open throughout.

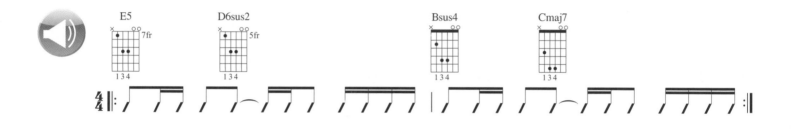

Drop D Tuning

Drop D tuning has become increasingly popular in all styles of guitar music. For drop D tuning, tune (drop) the sixth string down one whole step to the note D (instead of the regular E), leaving the rest of the strings tuned to standard tuning. The first and most obvious choice is to play an open D major chord, strumming all six strings and giving the chord a much fuller sound by utilizing a lower root note and 5th under the original chord. Of course, tuning one string differently disrupts all of the chords and fingerings you've already learned, but there are just as many benefits to drop D tuning, too. The example below shows a simple progression in drop D, using new chord diagrams for D major, E major, and G5.

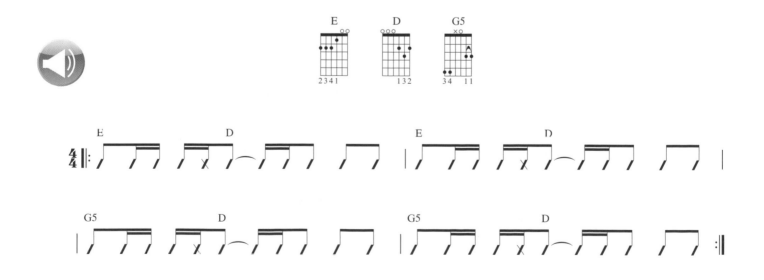

Drop D tuning is popular in heavy metal music because it allows you to play power chords with one finger and change chords at riff speed. Here's an example in tablature. Alternate between using your first, second, or third fingers to barre the two-note chords.

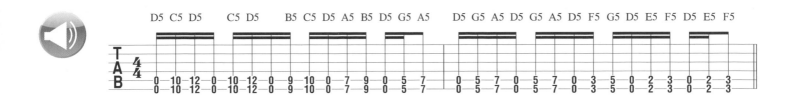

You've undoubtedly noticed by now that, in drop D tuning, all of the note names on the sixth string are different than they were in Chapter 5. Of course they are, because you've tuned the string differently. Here's another handy chart that shows the notes on the sixth string in drop D. It may be confusing at first, but if you play in drop D often enough, you'll soon get used to it.

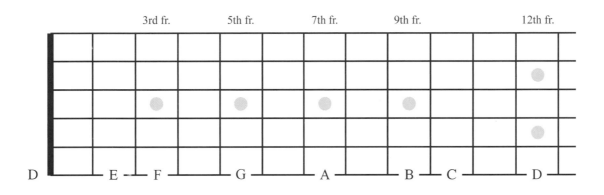

Drop D tuning also makes it easy to play big, sweeping power chords by combining the roots and 5ths in multiple octaves, a feat which is nearly impossible in standard tuning. Comparing the G5 frames below, you'll see that we can keep adding notes to make the chord even fuller. If you barre across all six strings, the first string will give you a 2nd, turning the chord into a sus2 chord.

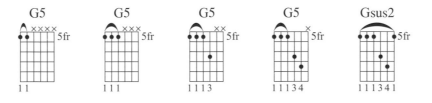

Capos

On a final note, you can use a movable clamp called a *capo* (pronounced *cay-po*) that will transpose the entire guitar in one shot. Capos are inexpensive gadgets that every guitarist should own. You can place it at any fret, essentially converting that fret into a nut, which will allow you to play the open chords at that position. Why would you need to do this if you can play barre chords? Because open chords really let the strings ring out and tend to sound fuller and bigger than the barre chords. You can combine the capo with open tunings or drop D tuning, too, and really open up the possibilities. Some popular frets to place the capo at are the second fret, third fret, fifth fret, and seventh fret, but a capo can be placed anywhere on the guitar. Try one out and begin experimenting.

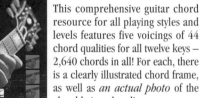
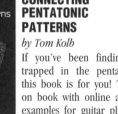